School

The Act of Mentoring:

Mentoring a Strongman for a Stronghold

Stirring Up, Activating and Imparting
Talents and Abilities for Effectiveness

By

Dr. Pauline Walley

Copyright © 2006 by Dr. Pauline Walley

School of Mentoring and Leadership I
The Act of Mentoring:
Mentoring a Strongman for a Stronghold;
Stirring Up, Activating and Imparting Talents
and Abilities for Effectiveness
by Dr. Pauline Walley

Printed in the United States of America

ISBN 1-60034-845-9

All rights reserved solely by the author. The author guarantees all contents are original and do not infringe upon the legal rights of any other person or work. No portion of this book may be reproduced, stored in a retrieval system, or transmitted in any form or by any other means—electronic, mechanical, photocopy, recording or any other—except for brief quotations in printed reviews—without the prior permission of the author. The views expressed in this book are not necessarily those of the publisher.

Unless otherwise indicated, Scripture references are from the New King James version of the Holy Bible. Copyright © 1990, 1985, 1983 by Thomas Nelson, Inc.

www.xulonpress.com

Contents

Introduction ix

Chapter One
    Understanding the Act of Mentoring 15
    What is mentoring? 17

Chapter Two
    Types of Mentoring: 19
        1. Intensive Mentoring 19
        2. Regular Mentoring 24
        3. Foundational Mentoring 28
        4. Occasional Mentoring 32
        5. Miraculous Mentoring 37

Chapter Three
    Who is a Mentor? 39

Chapter Four
    Who is Protégé? 53

Chapter Five
    Qualities 63
        a. Qualities of a Mentor 64
        b. Qualities of a Protégé 66

Chapter Six
    Responsibilities 73
        a. Responsibilities of a Mentor 74
        b. Choosing a Mentor 74
        c. Accepting a Protégé 75
        d. Responsibilities of a Protégé 75

Chapter Seven
    Relationship between a Mentor and
    a Protégé 77
        i. Fatherly 77
        ii. Motherly 79
        iii. Friendly 81

Chapter Eight
    Obstacles in Mentoring 85

Chapter Nine
    Dynamics of Mentoring 91
        i. Attraction 92
        ii. Responsiveness 94
        iii. Accountability 95

Chapter Ten
    Mentoring Strongmen for Strongholds 101

    School of Intensive Training 109
    Books by Dr. Pauline Walley 111
    Ministry Contacts 117

Acknowledgments

Special thanks to the Almighty God, who has put in me the spirit of humility to receive teaching and counsel through the power of the Holy Spirit.

Thanks to my parents Bishop Enoch and Felicia Walley and other members of my family for bringing me up in the fear of God. I hereby express my profound appreciation to the individuals who have stood with me at Overcomers' House and have encouraged me through my valleys and mountains with Pauline Walley Evangelistic Ministries.

These persons include: Rev. Peace Tackie, Minister Althia Rowe, Minister Makra Opoku, Deaconess Ebere Trotman, Deaconess Jessie Davies, Deaconess Monica Reyes, Deaconess

Rose Arloo, and Deaconess Ingrid Bedward. Others are Delta Thompson, Ngozi Kalu, Wise Doe and all Overcomers around the world.

Special thanks to Rev. Yvonne Richards, Thelma Nicholas, Rev. Solomon Tetteh and Albert Awadzi of London for coming on board to support this unique work around the world. I wish I could include all the names of my special lovers, supporters, and international coordinators, but time will not permit me to do so. However, I give thanks to all those who have contributed to the progressiveness of my life and ministry.

Special thanks to my *Unique Editor*, Kay Coulter, whose work and advice have been very inspiring and encouraging to me. My appreciation also goes to Dr. Kingsley Fletcher for accepting to validate my work and ministry.

Introduction

—〰—

During my doctorate program, one of the courses that I studied was "The Art of Mentoring." One of my research projects on this subject enabled me to interview several people within and around my ministry around the world.

By the end of my interactive aspect of the project, I was able to carve out a specific area of the research that will influence my work and ministry as an evangelist traveling the world. So I based my project on the "Dynamics of Mentoring."

This unique area of research defined my personal life and relationship with people that I encountered in my daily endeavors. I saw the need to be honest and committed to relationships that are either short term or long term.

Gradually, the wisdom gathered from this research began to affect my ministry, and I began to make impact in people's lives. Some of the people that I meet wherever I go, began to entrust their lives into my hand. Most of the people I meet call me "Mother" at the instant of meeting me. Some send me mails asking for permission to address me as "Mama or Mother" because I have imparted something unique into their lives.

In some society and communities, the adults call me "Mama" and the younger ones call me "Grandma." Before I went to the Philippines, all emails addressed me as "Mama Pauline." When I arrived at the Airport, I looked at the elderly persons "Pastor Conrado and Helen Sajonia" and I looked at the tiny me, and asked myself, do I deserve this great title? The term "Mama" is a great title. It is an honorable title accorded to people within whose hands you can entrust your life.

When Rev. Solomon Tetteh came to New York and addressed me as "Mama," New

Yorkers were shocked. Everybody became inquisitive and wanted to know my age. They also wanted to know if I was his biological mother. Rev. Solomon then explained the influence and the impact he had gained from my ministry and felt I deserve the title. Although, I hadn't had the opportunity to mentor them before they started to address me by that title, they saw the need and the desire to submit to my tutelage. Hence I accepted to work with them. Everywhere I go the story is the same.

Many people are yearning for relationships that would turn their lives around and give them a sense of belonging. Both men and women, young and old, boys and girls, youths and adult have been abused, assaulted and violated at one time or the other. Each of these persons needs to be supervised under a committed assurance that they can make it in life. Each of these individuals needs to be loved and accepted in the procedure that will help correct the misplaced foundations in their lives.

This book is not about an art or a theory but rather a practical demonstration of what mentoring will do for your life. We all need mentors. It does not matter who you are. Despite your achievements, you have a weakness that is bugging you like a cankerworm. The pastoral robe or the choir robe cannot heal the problem we have with our inabilities. Neither can the beautiful cloak nor a designer's suit kill the cankerworm hidden in our character, behavior and attitude. A mentoring relationship will do a good surgery and make us whole again by the grace of our Lord and Savior Jesus Christ.

Beloved, seek a mentoring relationship and submit yourself for correction, pruning and reconstruction, to strengthen your talents and abilities as they are being discovered. Seek and you shall find, knock and it shall be opened unto you, and your life shall never be the same.

This book will enlighten your eyes of understanding and enable you to understand the essence of mentoring and why you need it. Do not choose a mentor nor start the relationship until you have finished reading this book. You must understand the meaning and essence before you sign up for a relationship. Stay blessed and enjoy the unique blessing in this book.

Chapter One

Understanding the Act of Mentoring

Mentorship produces protégés, strongmen/women, quality businessmen/women, great entrepreneurs and potential leaders directly or indirectly.

Every mentor is not a leader and every leader is not a mentor. Many people have mistaken mentorship for leadership and leadership for mentorship, but the two activities are not the same and are not interchangeable. Similarly, a good mentor may not be a good leader and a good leader may not be a good mentor.

Mentorship and leadership are not the same, because some leaders are not willing to let a subordinate person rise above them. Some leadership will not allow another person to achieve a higher status even after they have retired and died. Also, there are mentors who are not willing to win their protégés, because they possess their protégés as servants and not as potential persons who should be given the freedom of independence to explore life on their own.

Many people in leadership position assume that they are mentors yet several of them have failed at home and in their responsibilities toward the people they lead and direct, hence such individuals cannot be considered as mentors at any level.

- A person who exhibits envy and jealousy cannot mentor anybody successfully.
- A person who is threatened by another person's ability to rise cannot mentor anyone successfully.

- A person who believes he or she is better than others cannot mentor others.
- A person who is proud and selfish cannot mentor successfully.
- A person who oppresses and frustrates others' promotion cannot mentor successfully.

What is mentoring?

Mentoring is a high level of impacting, equipping and building up both leaders and non-leaders to discover their potentials so that they can rise and shine as the bright morning star.

Mentoring is a process of helping another person to discover his/her God-given ability, in order for the one to step into his/her destiny and be fulfilled. Mentoring is also a process of helping an individual to build up himself/herself in order to acquire maturity to handle one's life endeavor. Mentoring is a process of assisting a person to stay focused on one's goal in order to achieve success.

Mentoring is like planting and tending a garden to ensure that each seed sown is well groomed to receive adequate impetus that generates fruitfulness and multiplication (Genesis 1:28 and Psalm 1).

In Genesis 2:19, God mentored Adam when He gave Adam the opportunity to demonstrate the ability that had been imparted unto mankind.

Chapter Two

Types of Mentoring

Mentoring can be divided into five groups: Intensive Mentoring, Regular Mentoring, Foundational Mentoring, Occasional Mentoring and Miraculous Mentoring.

1. **Intensive Mentoring**
    Spiritual Guardianship
        Mentoring
    Organizational Mentoring
    Discipleship Mentoring

Intensive mentoring
Intensive mentoring is a process of planning a specific training program to raise certain individuals to go on a mission or to occupy a

position in an organization. It is a process of raising people to carry on a particular vision in order to achieve a specific or mandated goal within a season or a time frame.

Intensive mentoring focuses on training and impacting a vision for a mission, and it has a direct impartation on the protégé. Intensive mentoring includes: Spiritual guidance, Discipleship, and Coaching.

Spiritual Mentoring

Spiritual mentoring is a process of assisting an individual or a young Christian to develop his/her faith. A *Spiritual mentor is one who guides a person's spiritual life so* that one can understand the essence of the Christian faith and develop a Christ-like character.

Proverbs 13:20 – "He who walks with wise men will be wise . . ." therefore every mentor must also have a mentor because no one is above correction. A mentor also needs another mentor for the purpose of accountability and to maintain checks and balances in a mentor's behavior and presentation.

Spiritual Mentoring for Ministry

Spiritual mentoring is a process of sharing a divine vision with other persons, so that the vision could be received and supported by others. The intention of spiritual mentoring is to enable a divinely endowed vision to be rooted for fruitfulness and multiplication.

In spiritual mentoring, the mentor intends to raise followers to join force with him/her in order to gain continuity and expansion. In this type of mentoring, the protégé is expected to serve the mentor for life.

The protégé is also expected to be a part and a branch of the main vision. The protégé's vision must therefore conform to the mentor's vision, and the protégé must be willing to submit his/her vision to the mentor for engraftment into the core vision and mission; otherwise there will later be a split or division in the organization because the vision differs.

Organizational Mentoring

Organizational mentors organize seminars or training programs to build up their protégés so that the organization's vision can be strengthened through the input and support of protégés.

Discipleship Mentoring

Just like spiritual mentoring, discipleship mentoring is focused on imparting a spiritual knowledge and faith based principles into a person or a group of people through training. The purpose is to equip and empower the disciples to create fruitfulness and multiplication to advance the faith concerned.

Discipleship is spiritually oriented and the intention is to advance a faith based or religious concept, whereby the discipline of a religion is spelt out and enumerated for others to imbibe and practice.

Also, discipleship is multiplication. Therefore disciples must be able to teach others what they have been taught. Discipleship could be direct or indirect (Matthew 28:19-20). Jesus Christ concentrated on discipling twelve persons. However, there were silent disciples among the multitudes who were silent observers. These silent disciples emulated the lifestyle and teaching of Christ Jesus, some of whom later became writers of the gospel of Jesus Christ.

Regular Mentoring
Parental Mentoring
Sibling Mentoring
Friendship Mentoring

Regular mentors are the people with whom we live and relate in our daily endeavors. They are people who are close to us either by birth, adoption or familiarity. Regular mentors include parents, siblings, companions, friends, and people who are directly involved in our lives.

Every parent has an opportunity to become a natural mentor; however, every parent is not a mentor. Some parents are friends to their children while some do not know how to relate to their wards. Likewise, siblings are supposed to be play assistantship to one another; unfortunately, there are siblings that do not relate well, so they do not share their visions, dreams and aspirations among themselves.

Interestingly, there are friends who function as mentors to everyone around them. A friend to one family member can turn out to be a mentor to the whole family.

Parental Mentoring

Every parent is not a mentor, even as everyone does not understand the meaning and importance of mentoring. A parent may be a mentor, but to other persons, and not to his/her own wards. A parent who is a mentor will diligently seek to mentor his/her own wards as though, he/she is dealing with an outsider.

Some parents are able to discover their wards' unique abilities and assist them to develop such, while others are not able to do so. Besides discovering a child's ability, there is also a need to assist the proper management of that which has been discovered. A parent who is not a mentor may not know the importance of the unique abilities that is embedded in his/her family.

Sibling Mentoring

Siblings are biological children from the same parents. There are children of the same family who are privileged to act as mentors to each member of the family. Such abilities are traits of natural mentorship. Some natural mentors do not often know that they are performing the act until they are identified or recognized by others.

Siblings who are mentors take time to coach other members of the family. They help their brothers and sisters to recognize their talents and work with them until they are able to manage their abilities.

Irrespective of age or qualification attained, a sibling who is a natural mentor would give other members of the family a natural support.

Friendship Mentoring

There are relationships that make a person, and there are relationships that lead to the discovering of one's destiny. Relationships like friendship can be very beneficial to the individuals involved.

Friendship is an art of adopting an acquaintance or alliance with somebody that can be trusted. A friend is a companion with whom one shares and discusses matters that affect one's daily endeavors without the fear of intimidation or betrayal. There are childhood friends who are well kept for life; and there are adult friends and others who were adopted as life situations and circumstances permit.

No matter how a friendship was initiated, sometimes a friend may act like a mentor by discovering one's ability and also providing useful assistance to nurture and groom the talents concerned.

Foundational Mentoring
Mentoring in Teaching
Mentoring in Coaching
Mentoring Students

Foundational Mentoring for Educational Orientation

In order for some people to be successful in their academic endeavors, they will need mentors with whom to discuss their abilities and ambitions. Sometimes a person's ability does not conform to the ambition that one intends to pursue in life. When a person's ability differs from his/her ambition, the person's efforts may later become stagnant and his/her ambition becomes unfulfilled.

In some cases, parental ambition and control could undermine a person's vision. Hence a mentor is needed to examine a person's educational orientation for there to be a successful carrier and academic orientation.

Foundational mentoring helps a child to coordinate his academic work with his talents in order to build up his/her future ambitions coherently. Foundational mentoring includes: mentoring in teaching, mentoring in coaching and mentoring students.

Mentoring in Teaching

Teaching is the process of educating in order to enable a person to understand the basic principles that are needed for one to apply knowledge to a thinking process. A teacher is not necessarily a mentor; however, the act and performance of a teacher could provide a mentoring opportunity for a student.

A teacher who has a motherly or fatherly instinct could be a good mentor to students. Thus, a teacher with a strong parental instinct could go beyond just teaching but also showing concern for the potential ability of a student.

A teacher who is able to discover and nurture a student to succeed beyond academic achievement is a mentor. Therefore it is possible to provide a mentoring situation in a classroom setting or within a teaching atmosphere.

Mentoring as Coaching

A coach is a person who motivates and imparts skills.

A coach is someone who helps an individual to develop his talent skillfully. Mentoring in coaching is the process of helping a person to skillfully develop his/her potentials for a successful venture. It is a process of training that polishes an individual's ability in order to become a master of a trade or vocation.

Mentoring Students

There are academic institutions that provide mentoring facilities for students. In such an environment where mentoring is considered as a curriculum vitae, students are privileged to receive a direct mentoring program which enables them to discover their hidden abilities and also build a purposeful ambition around their profession.

Student mentoring helps to eliminate bogus ambitions and unfulfilled dreams that may lead to wasted years. Mentoring students eliminates unnecessary youthful exuberances and creates room for excavations of hidden treasures. Students mentoring centers are where great potentials are developed at early stages of life, and unique abilities and talents are discovered.

Occasional Mentoring
Counselors
Teachers
Supervisors
Colleagues
Sponsors

Occasional mentors are people who are not directly related to us, but they are involved in our daily endeavors on official levels. Thus we are affiliated to occasional mentors by virtue of fulfilling our official or academic duties. Occasional mentors are involved in our lives by virtue of our daily endeavors. They are not biologically related or family friends. Occasional mentors include colleagues at work, schoolmates, teachers, sponsors and supervisors.

Counselors Mentoring

A counselor is someone who gives a therapeutic advice to people. Some educational institutions provide counseling facilities for students. Although the role of the educational counselor is to assist students with career guidance, they have also acted as mentors at crucial moments. However, in the process of dealing with students over the years, some counselors have developed mentoring skills to enhance their duties and performances.

Teachers Mentoring

Teachers are educational facilitators. Although there are different types of teachers at various levels, yet besides academic orientation, teachers may act as mentors who discover and develop individual students' abilities.

For instance, my dad is a teacher but not a mentor. When one of my brothers started school, immediately, one of his teachers discovered his talents and the area of interest being engineering. The teacher then invited my dad for a discussion that was meant to develop his talents towards his ambition and enhance my brother's future in relation to his interest and career. Letters were also written to report the activities of my brother while in school—thus my brother was interested in science and engineering. He would spend the break hours fixing equipment that the school could not afford to put in place.

Although my dad was an educationalist, he was not a mentor, so he did not act upon the reports he had received. All that my dad wanted was just to provide academic education for his children. He did not understand the importance of facilitating one's talents and abilities. He also did not consider the importance of blending early learning with a person's talents and abilities.

In view of this shortcoming in my dad, my brother could not live up to expectations, and he is disappointed that he was not trained in the area of his interest, which is engineering.

Supervisor Mentoring

Some people went to work not because they wanted to but because of challenges beyond their control. Some others went to work in order to fulfill their destiny, but they have not been able to work with their professional achievements; they are in occupations that only help to provide their daily bread and pay bills.

People who are occupied with jobs that do not fulfill their desires and career ambitions usually feel frustrated and disappointed in life. They feel as though they have failed and find it difficult to forgive themselves. There are people who do not know what will actually make them and so wander around until the opportunity comes for them to discover themselves.

Job supervisors who are sharp in their reasoning, and those who are natural mentors, have often discovered talents on the job. Some of these talents are recommended for training and promoted to fulfill their destiny by their employers.

Some business organizations identify the importance of mentoring. Hence they provide training facilities for persons with unique abilities who are discovered on the job, both to the advantage of the organization and to the satisfaction of the workers concerned.

Colleague Mentoring

Colleagues are fellow workers on the job. There are job colleagues who are either trained or natural mentors. They provide relational mentoring for fellow workers with the intention to help or assist the individuals. Although the role of such mentoring colleagues may not be recognized by the business organization where he/she works, this unique gifting could be an asset from which all friendly workers and their family members could benefit.

In some instances they are recognized and accepted to fulfill that role by the organization with which they work.

Sponsorship Mentoring

There are business organizations, institutions and individual philanthropists who engage in sponsoring young talents by providing financial assistance for their trainings. Thus these sponsors set aside some funding for developing young talents in a certain area of training, besides academic achievements.

Miraculous Mentoring
Accidental Mentors
Divine Encounter
The Good Samaritan

Miraculous mentors are not chosen but are run into. They are usually unplanned for but are led by circumstances that are not designed by human factors. Miraculous mentoring includes accidental mentoring, divine encounter mentoring and the Good Samaritan mentoring.

Accidental Mentoring

Accidental mentoring is unplanned for and was never expected. It was by coincidence. It just happened.

Divine Encounter Mentoring

Divine encounter mentoring is simply God's intervention. God uses His discretion to step into a matter and provide assistance where one could not have ever expected that it could ever be possible. It is a case where God in His miraculous move reveals a case to a mentor to take up the responsibility of mentoring a specific protégée to ensure that person's development.

The Good Samaritan Mentoring

The Good Samaritan Mentoring means somebody decided to help in order to save a situation. There are people who offer to help others with their talents and abilities voluntarily. Even if it is not convenient, they offer to assist in situations that need to be rescued. Such people are known as Good Samaritan.

Chapter Three

Who is a Mentor?

A mentor is a person who is able to build a relationship with a protégée with the intention to help discover the talents that he/she possesses, and also provide opportunities for the protégée to develop his/her skills. A mentor is not necessarily a leader because all leaders do not produce protégés.

A mentor is a person who has been able to attain remarkable achievements in his/her life endeavors. A mentor's achievements serve as a good example to others. A mentor is a type of a hero or model that everyone seems to look up to and desires to emulate because of the quality of their characteristics and unique performances.

A mentor is a wise and trusted advisor.

A mentor is one who can be emulated or replicated.

A mentor is one who can guide, tutor, counsel or advise.

A mentor is one who can help others develop their talents and unique abilities.

Mentoring is a process of taking one's gifts, abilities and talents and sharing them with others.

Mentoring is also the process of discovering other persons' abilities and helping them to develop such to become fruitful.

Mentoring is the ability to reproduce one's fruitfulness in others.

Protégés learn the act of mentoring from their mentors.

Protégés are bound to reproduce whatever concepts they learned from previous mentors.

The purpose of mentoring is not to produce a carbon copy of the mentor in the protégée. In the realms where mentoring has been misunderstood and misplaced for discipleship, some (ignorant) leaders have tried to reproduce themselves in their supporters and followers in assumption of mentoring others.

Where mentoring has been misunderstood, consciously or unconsciously, a mentor is either disseminating information into a protégé through cloning and duplicating, or by replicating and imitating. At a certain level, a mentor may impart his own skills on a protégé either consciously or unconsciously. This usually happens in cases where the mentor is seeking discipleship and the protégé is a younger person or a teenager.

A mentor should not practice any of the following: cloning or duplicating oneself in another. This is because:

Cloning

Cloning in mentoring **is not acceptable**. Cloning is an attempt to reproduce oneself in a protégé irrespective of the consequences in one's nature or characteristics. Cloning is duplicating both the good and bad character in a person.

A person who believes that everything he/she has and does is alright, therefore his protégé must not be any different than himself/herself is not a mentor but a mere leader seeking followers.

Duplication

Duplicating in mentoring **is a wrong concept**. It means to repeat the exact identity of the existing abilities or qualities from one person to an intending protégé. It is a process where a supposed mentor believes his/her protégé must be like him/her—an identical twin of oneself.

A mentor may adapt any of the following to enhance progress: Replication, Imitation or Emulation.

Replication

Replication is not a wrong concept in mentoring, if only the mentor focuses on the protégé's ability. Replicating is to produce a better copy of oneself in another. The mentor is able to repeat his/her performance by reproducing a better quality of himself/herself in a protégé, but not necessarily instilling his/her her copy in another person.

Imitation

Imitation is to follow a pattern or procedure in possessing some of the attributes of a mentor. Thus a mentor is supposed to be a model for a protégé to emulate some unique attributes that he/she possesses, in addition to what already exists in a protégé's life, as an additional factor for improvement in mentoring development. The mentor's attribute is a developmental pattern for achieving and managing success.

Emulation

Emulation is a good concept to imbibe in mentoring. Emulation is an attempt to equal or excel above a model. Emulation gives a protégé the opportunity to perform a discovered skill with success, without being hindered by a mentor.

Types of Mentors

There are different types of mentors just as there are different types of mentoring in different areas of life, as discussed in the early chapters of this book. The nature of an individual is a factor and has an impact in mentoring procedure. Similarly, the cultural background and level of education as well as understanding of the concept of mentoring have an impact in the life of mentors.

The gender factor of mentoring could be very interesting, as people tend to do things according to their natural disposition. A man trained by a single mother will often have a trait of a female behavior and a lady who grew up among boys will turn out to be a tomboy, therefore her perception of things would be from a masculine perception.

a. Men as Mentors

Some men are very strong and masculine in nature, and some are sensitive, yet masculine in their behavior. On the other hand, some men are strong but have some feminine attributes and some men just behave like women in all their endeavors.

Irrespective of one's natural gender, there are some attributes in a male that makes him a father or a mother figure even if one has no biological children. Whenever this unique attribute occur, a male tends to have a feminine heart or a compassionate heart. That male does not behave in a feminine way outwardly, but thinks like a mother and not a woman. (***Please note that this has nothing to do with lesbianism or homosexuality***).

Thinking like a mother means a man has a compassionate heart. He is very emotional and is concerned about the well-being of people around. Men with motherly hearts carry the problems of others in their bosoms like a pregnancy and groan with them in prayer until success is born. It means that man with a motherly heart listens carefully and prayerfully considers the endeavors of a protégé with deep heart intercession, seeking the future of the protégé with a passion.

The man with a fatherly heart seeks a sense of belonging in a protégé rather than granting him/her an independent role to function in his/her skills. A man with a fatherly heart does not believe his boy can survive or succeed without him. He wants to be involved in everything done by the protégé and feels a little insecure when the protégé exercises decision without his consent.

A male mentor will usually look at things from a fatherly perspective and give advice in that regard.

b. Women as Mentors

Girls who are born in the midst of challenges and are left to fend for themselves often turn out to be very masculine in their way of life and thoughts. Their characteristics can be aggressive and masculine, often on the warring side of life. Even when they are not facing challenges, they tend to be on the defensive and always ready to resume the battle.

Although women in this category may be wives or mothers in the practical sense of it, yet they do not operate in the emotional realm. Such women are often too strong and they even expect young ones to be as strong as themselves. They are not sensitive to the emotions of other people.

Masculine women are often very militant mentors. They do well with coaching but are not very good with giving instructions. They tend to enforce directives instead of giving instructions that will help to develop a skill.

c. Youth Mentors

There are two types of youth mentors — a peer mentor and a young-adult (senior) mentor.

A youth mentor would usually relate to a protégé who is a peer on a friendship level, rather than on authority level. In an academic setting like a high school, peers may have the opportunity to mentor others. The individuals in an upper class considered as seniors may choose to mentor someone in a lower class, such as juniors.

A senior person mentoring a junior may do it more on a supervisory level. At this level, where there is understanding of its importance, the emotional factors (the fatherly and motherly spirit) are quickly noted and developed. Otherwise some youths would tease and bully a person who has a unique emotional ability instead of appreciating it.

Individuals should not be discouraged to exhibit their emotional attributes during mentoring but must learn to control and manage habits that tend to disrupt good skills—such as emotions that display fatherly or mother expressions in mentoring.

d. Inspirational Mentors

Inspirational mentors are people we admire for their tenacity and achievements. Inspirational mentors are mentors vicariously. We cannot get to them, yet we admire their attributes from afar and we follow their programs by reading, watching or attending their programs. For instance, although Michael Jackson the singer and the late Princess of Wales, Lady Diana and Oprah Winfrey may not be known as *born again* Christians, yet they are models that a lot of people admire and pay attention to. I love them for their consistency in managing their success and the impact they have made around the world. Although some of the reports we hear may not be too good, yet, they have made great inroads in their destinies.

Nevertheless, since the act of mentoring involves impartation, it is wise for Christians to seek mentors who are persons of good reputation, full of the Holy Spirit and wisdom (**Acts 6:3**). Integrity should be the core of our search for mentors, and not worldliness (**Genesis 6:9**).

e. Chosen Mentors

A chosen mentor is one who is specifically chosen to help an inexperienced person to polish up his skills and gain much experience for advancement.

One may be attracted to choose a particular person as a mentor because of an identical skill that the person has. A protégé may decide to choose a particular person as a mentor because he/she can recognize a need for a special skill. In order for that protégé to move on to another level, he/she may need the supervision or advice of a successful person in that realm. Chosen mentors must be blameless and good stewards of God (Titus 1:5-9).

f. Adventurous Mentors

An adventurous mentor is a risk taker. He/she is one who takes risks to mentor someone in dire need of skillful development. The risk may involve life or financial demands, yet an adventurous mentor is willing to assist.

g. Professional Mentors

Professional mentors are trained mentors whose official employment is based on mentoring people. Professional mentors sometimes occupy the office of a counselor in some organizations. Some paralegal personnel also act as professional mentors as they provide technical advice to clients on a regular basis.

The things that motivate one to seek a mentor include:

    i. Quality of production and presentation

ii. Moral values (public behavior and presentation)
iii. Character, behavior and attitude

Chapter Four

Who Is a Protégé?

A protégé is a person who willingly submits himself/herself for mentoring. Thus until a person sees the need to be helped and subscribes for assistance to be mentored, the person will not be able to occupy the position of a protégé. A protégé is often not chosen, but a mentor is always chosen.

Anybody occupying any position in life should consider submitting to a mentoring relationship. A person occupying the position of a president of a nation can submit to mentoring during his term of office. Thus a current president should be able to submit to a past president for mentoring irrespective of political differences and opposition songs that are sung during political campaigns.

It is important that a political aspirant submits to a mentoring relationship under former political leaders in order to learn from past mistakes. President Bill Clinton was known to have referred to Ex-President Jimmy Carter as a father and a mentor during his term of office (*not sure of the date – but heard it on a television program*).

For a person to be successful in a leadership position or managerial office, it is wise to seek the counsel of an advisor who is able to correct and mentor one without fear of intimidation or betrayal. Every leadership position demands a need for a mentor, a counselor and an advisor. A personal mentor can be retained privately, besides official and state advisors who may be performing their professional duties. Sometimes professional performances may be deceptive because professional work may fulfill their official responsibilities but not necessarily to satisfy a client.

King David had official advisors and mentors. Samuel the prophet served as his mentor. Zadok, Abiathar and Ahithophel were among the priests who functioned as the official administrative counselors in the king's court. Ahithophel later conspired to join the camp of Absalom (2 Samuel 15:29-31).

Nathan was a personal prophet and counselor to King David. He remained a faithful mentor and prophetic advisor till the very end. Nathan was the prophet who pointed out King David's error when he committed adultery. Nathan was the same prophet who engineered the installation of Solomon as King of Judah, having noted the struggles among the other children in the palace (1 Kings 1:22-27, 38).

In this case, Nathan the mentor submitted to his protégé who was occupying a higher position of authority. Each party respected each other's position and office, so at crucial times, there was no problem with noting an error and effecting correction. Nathan was always pointing out errors to King David, and the king always listened to Nathan's advice.

Men as Protégés

Many men need the attention of a mentoring relationship to become accountable and responsible fathers. Many men have failed in fulfilling their roles as husbands of wives (one man to one woman) and father of their own children.

- Some men have failed in their educational endeavors and need to be mentored to overcome their pasts.
- Some men have never lived under the authority of a father and have never tasted fatherhood in their lives, so they were brought up under the tutelage of females—from mother to grandmother or to auntie, so they feel life has failed them. How are they expected to know what it means to respond to authority or keep a home?
- Some men have failed in their ability to gain promotions on the job and feel death is the end result of their failures.

- Some men have been abused by situations and circumstances that they think cannot be mended or corrected.
- Some men are intimidated because their wives or children are doing better than they have ever done.
- Some men are insecure because their spouses are better read than they are.
- Some men are brokenhearted (wounded lions) because they were corrected or rebuked by somebody.
- Some men feel rejected because their talents have not been recognized and accepted.
- Some men are deflated because no one has ever acknowledged or validated their good works.
- Some men need another man to lift their heads up through mentoring.

Men in general need mentoring in all endeavors to successfully manage their homes in addition to their professional and public achievements. Many men cannot manage their success. Their achievements have led them into sins such as pride, adultery, secret cults and all manner of indulgence that attracts spiritual wickedness in high places.

Women as Protégés

The destiny of many women has been limited to marriage and childbearing. Hence when their marriage is without childbearing, they are relegated to ordinary bed partners or table/kitchen partners.

Women are intelligent beings created from the secret of a man's heart. The woman is the strength of a man and the vitality of his existence. Therefore the secret of a man's success is in the heart and soul of a woman.

Women equally need mentoring relationships to fulfill their destiny. The woman is the pillar of success behind every wise man. Therefore women need mentoring to understand their role in marriage and in the life of their husbands. Women need mentoring to understand how to assist and manage the secret of their husbands' lives.

Women are created to function as the divine helpmates and inspiration that motivates success in home building and family life. Without mentoring, many pregnancies are aborted because of fear of failure.

Through a mentoring relationship:

- A woman will learn to motivate her husband into success.
- A woman will learn to nurture her pregnancy to maturation.
- A woman will learn to manage her pains in pregnancies instead of resorting to abortion.
- A woman will learn to manage her birth pains and sustain the life of her children to maturation.
- A woman will learn to uproot bitterness from her heart and give her children love.
- A woman will never consider herself as a slave in her own home.
- A woman will never allow herself to be relegated to nothing.

- A woman will walk with her shoulders lifted high among others.
- A woman will consider herself as highly favored among others.

Many women are highly talented, but because of childhood abuse and assault, their abilities have been crippled. For women who have been violated and assaulted by family members, friends and strangers, there is need for mentoring relationship besides counseling.

Youth Protégés

The destinies of many children are limited by either the financial well-being of their parents or the backgrounds and academic opinions of their guardians. Some children are not able to pursue their ambition because of the myopic thinking of their guardians. Parents who are easily intimidated feel insecure when their wards begin to express high opinions and desires for great ambitions.

In the case where parents are not open to development and creativity, the parents need counseling to release their wards for mentoring. There are parents who are intimidated when other people try to help or assist their wards. These kind of intimidating attitudes and insecurity destroy the hope and aspirations of youths.

Foundational mentoring relationships provided through the early school system could help remove some of the fears expressed by insecure parents and guardians.

Inspirational Protégés

People who are humble at heart and teachable always desire to learn more. Such people are inspirational protégés to great men and women by vicarious involvement because of their willingness to submit to learning.

Chosen Protégés

When a protégé is chosen, the person may not submit to the total expectation of the mentor. This may sever the relationship between the two persons, as the choice was not based on the desire of the protégé.

Adventurer Protégés

Some people are risk takers and may decide to submit to a person whom they do not like. Thus the protégé just wants the assistance of the mentor to fulfill a need for a short time, but he/she is actually not interested in other matters, hence they depart immediately once the assignment is completed.

Chapter Five

Qualities of a Mentor and Protégé

1. Ability to set goals and monitor them
2. Ability to maintain achievements
3. Ability to reproduce self without fear of threat
4. Ability to listen attentively
5. Ability to supervise
6. Ability to make corrections without bruising
7. Ability to re-examine an issue
8. Ability to give credit
9. Ability to observe correction and affect it
10. Ability to condescend to protégé's level for help

11. **Ability to welcome and facilitate new ideas**
12. **Not being manipulative**
13. **Not covering up personal weaknesses**
14. **Avoiding fault finding and blame shifting**
15. **Decipher between when to pray and when to counsel**
16. **Not intimidating**
17. **Not envious**
18. **Not jealous**
19. **Not competitive**
20. **Not humiliating**
21. **No hidden agenda**

Qualities of a Mentor

- A mentor is one who communicates and allows communication flow in a relationship.
- A mentor is one who allows interaction in a relationship without the fear of intimidation.
- A mentor is one who is able to live by example.

- A mentor is one who is able to submit to another mentor, because no one is above correction.
- This is to foster checks and balances and also for the purpose of accountability.
- A mentor is one who is able to give credit to good performances as a means of encouragement.
- A mentor is one who is able to sacrifice self for the benefit of a protégé.
- A mentor is one who accepts mistakes and initiates correction.
- A mentor does not force his will on a protégé.
- A mentor does not often choose his protégé.

The sharp qualities of a mentor also reflect in his performances:

- Ability to identify the talents in a protégée
- Ability to motivate the talents to develop
- Ability to help the talent to grow

- Ability to foster the destiny of a protégé by counseling, instructing, and encouraging.

Qualities of a Protégé

i. Submissive to teachings

One of the reasons a protégé is allowed to choose his/her mentor is because there has to be a great level of respect and submission between the two. There has to be a good level of communication flow. And the two people going into a mentoring relationship must be in love and must cherish one another (1 John 4:7-8). Without an iota of love, a mentoring relationship cannot be successful.

Willing to be instructed: A person seeking a mentoring relationship must be willing to receive instructions. Jesus gave the disciples special instructions that would enable them to carry out the gospel after he had ascended into heaven (Acts 1:14). In the New Testament we see that Peter and others were able to receive power to preach, teach and perform unique miracles because they obeyed the instructions given to them (Acts 2). Mentoring is predominantly an instructive procedure. The essence of seeking mentoring is to receive special instruction to help build up one's abilities and polish up skills for a better life. Therefore a protégé must choose a person from whom one can receive instruction without fear of intimidation.

Willing to be directed: Similarly, a person seeking a mentoring relationship must understand the meaning of direction. Noah was able to build God an ark that led to the deliverance of his family and himself and even other creatures because he understood the impact of following directions (Genesis 6).

The repercussion of ignoring mentoring directions could be the same as ignoring divine directions. Sometimes, a mentor is God chosen, but we do not realize it because we are prone to disobedience and set in our own ways. It is very important that a person seeking a mentoring relationship considers the importance of the intricacies of the mentoring.

Willing to be corrected: The Scripture says "He who spares his rod hates his son, but he who loves him disciplines him promptly" (Proverbs 13:24). The Bible also states that God prunes those whom He loves. Many people are perishing because they do not know or understand the importance of correction. Many relationships are broken and many homes are destroyed because nobody wants to be corrected.

Correction brings healing, and healing brings restoration. One of the focuses of mentoring is to receive correction wherever one has gone wrong and make amendments for better construction of life. If a foundation is faulty, it must be open to correction, if the foundation refuses correction, then the structure will not stand the test of time. It will collapse and an important investment would be destroyed with it.

Life is a structure. Our abilities and talents are like structures that need to be placed on strong foundations. The foundations we need for these abilities and talents are instructions, directives and corrections. If our attitude to submission is wrong, then our abilities and talents will face frustration and we may never be fulfilled. We may be living in our destiny, yet there will be no joy of satisfaction.

ii. Submissive to authority

Submission to authority is the core foundation of mentoring. A mentoring relationship depends on submission to authority as a foundation for building a fruitful, fulfilling and successful relationship. Submission to authority is important, because once you call for mentoring relationship, you are asking for an authority to assist you to achieve a purposeful goal in life. At that point, you have to surrender your position and humbly receive through a relationship which will renew and shape your focus for good.

Acting respectful and obedient: A mentoring is an act that demands respect and obedience. You must willingly and voluntarily respect and obey the authority of your mentor, even if he/she is not well-educated or wealthy financially. Note that the person is wealthy in knowledge and skillfulness; that is why you chose him for a mentor (Daniel 1).

Willing to be pruned: Pruning means to cut off or to trim the dead part of something that has life or ability to grow. Part of the process of mentoring seeks to prune the dead part of a person's life, so that the protégé can grow successfully.

A person seeking mentoring must learn to counsel and advise himself/herself before going into a mentoring relationship. That person must make a strong decision not to quit when he/she comes into a place called pruning. Note that pruning is biblical and essential for development.

Willing to be rebuked: Rebuke simply means to put a stop to that which is not functioning well. Correction means something has gone wrong, and an error has occurred, therefore there is a need to straighten up the course of action. Pruning means a type of death has occurred in the process of a growth and development, therefore the death ends need to be trimmed.

These three factors—rebuke, correction and pruning—if well applied, help a farmer to achieve a successful harvest. These same factors are the strengths of a person who is capable of mentoring another person. Therefore, anyone seeking a mentoring relationship must be aware of these factors.

Samson failed in his destiny because he did not obey divine instruction and directives, as they were given to his parents even before his conception. Samson arrogated himself above the law of the land and also ignored the commandment that forbids an Israelite from getting into a marriage relationship with ungodly persons. Samson destroyed his destiny and himself by his own behavior and utterances he made.

A protégé must learn the wisdom of submission and obedience and must consider humility as a key point to success before stepping into a mentoring relationship with any person.

Chapter Six

Responsibilities

Mentoring has a lot of responsibilities and accountabilities. Initiating a mentoring relationship is like going into a higher institution of learning. In another realm it is like initiating a marital relationship. One does not quit college because a teacher is not understandable. However, one has a choice to conduct an inquiry into the capabilities of the teachers in an institution before signing up for admission. But it would be an act of insubordination for a student to query or investigate a teacher after he/she has been admitted.

It is very important for each of the parties going into a mentoring relationship to investigate one another and draw up important queries to erase all doubts before signing up for the relationship. Do not assume that things will be alright before you start. Note that the two parties have responsibilities in the relationship. Each must be aware of his/her role.

a. Responsibilities of a Mentor: The mentor's immediate responsibilities which are the core of the role of a mentor are: to groom, to develop, to build, to enhance and to transform a protégé's life and skills or abilities.

The mentor must then set up an agenda that will help to focus on the aims and objectives of a particular relationship. Each mentoring relationship must have a specific agenda. Although the principles of mentoring are the same, yet each protégé must be encouraged to submit an agenda relating to his/her purpose.

b. Choosing a Mentor: Before a mentor is chosen, a protégé must be able to define his purpose and objective. The protégé must be willing to share his vision and career objectives with the mentor. It is also very important that the protégé shares his area of weakness and strength so that the mentor will be able to apply the factors of submission effectively. During the process of negotiating a mentoring relationship, the protégé must pay attention to the level of communication flow. The protégé must ensure the effective communication and adequate dialogue without a fear of betrayal, insecurity or dishonesty.

c. Accepting a Protégé: Similarly, the mentor must consider the level of sincerity and honesty in the tone of the initial conversation to ensure that the protégé is ready to submit to the relationship.

Both parties must understand and acceptance the responsibilities involved in the process of mentoring.

d. Responsibilities of a Protégé: The protégé must set his/her own goals and the targets that one expects to meet by a certain period. The protégé must present initiatives that the mentor is expected to work with.

The protégé must note that the mentor is a helper and not the initiator of his visions and ambitions. The mentor is to help to enhance and strengthen what the protégé already has.

Chapter Seven

Relationship between a Mentor and a Protégé

The relationship between a mentor and a protégé is as important as one between a husband and a wife or a father and son/mother and daughter. The mentoring relationship is not one of a master and servant or a leader and a subordinate. Instead, it is like one between a shepherd and a sheep (John 10:1-30) if related to mentoring for discipleship.

i. Fatherly Relationship

In many society mentors are referred to as fathers—such as father of a nation, father of an organization or father of a good course.

Some mentors are referred to as fathers not because they are leaders but because their fatherly advice and counsel has helped to reconstruct and shape many lives.

Mentoring is instruction oriented (protective and caring): Although mentoring is instruction oriented, yet a mentor with a father's heart is protective and caring.

Rules and Regulations Conscious: A mentor who is very masculine usually is very conscious of the rules and regulations that bind the relationship, rather than being loving and persuasive. A mentor must be soft at heart and persuasive enough to win the heart of the protégé with a spirit of encouragement.

Pruning and Correcting: As much as mentoring consists of pruning and correcting, the mentor must seeking a loving and persuasive approach in order not to destroy the good work that is being constructed. A mentor with a masculine approach to life may prune and correct with an iron hand, and that may destroy the love that is supposed to be generated in the relationship.

Understanding: Understanding is a major factor in mentoring. Misunderstanding may lead to misinformation and misinformation may also lead to misconception. Therefore, there is a need for each of the parties to submit to one another by giving one another opportunities to ask questions and to cross-examine information.

The masculine factor must be played down for peace and love to reign in the relationship. For instance, many wives cannot ask their husbands questions because of the masculine factor. Interrogation in certain relationships is an act of disrespect or insubordination.

Supportive: A mentor must lay down his personal principles and show a fatherly support for the protégé's vision. The mentor must also show a great level of genuine interest in the vision and aspirations for which the protégé is seeking mentorship.

ii. Motherly Relationship

Mentoring relationship is motherly oriented because it demands motherly affection. The demand for motherly affection is not feminine or masculine related, but rather it is spirit and soul related. Thus a sincere mother does not throw away a child because the child misbehaved. Even when a child is incarcerated or jailed for wrongdoing, the mother seeks all means to reach out to her child. The love of a mother does not seek the destruction of a child, even if the child is disabled (1 Kings 3:16-28). Meanwhile many men with masculine ideas have left home because they cannot stand the crying and screaming of a child or the chirpy, chirpy noise of children.

Feeding: A mentor with a motherly spirit is concerned about the feeding of a protégé. This feeding is not the consumption of edible material but rather the consumption of knowledge and its application. The mentor shows concern for the progress of the protégé. The expression for feeding is like that of a mother breastfeeding a child.

Nurturing: A mentor with a motherly spirit will ensure that the provision of nutrients helps the growth of the protégé. Thus the mentor must provide some basic information that will assist the protégé to understand the key factors that will foster and influence the development of his personality besides his talents and abilities.

Tendering: A mentor must have a tendering spirit. He or she also must be caring.

Devotional: A mentor must be ready to devote a quality time to the protégé like a nursing mother would to a precious baby.

Maternalistic: Like a mother nursing a baby in a maternity ward, so is a mentor. A mentor must be conscious of the baby that he/she is nursing and must handle the protégé with care.

i. <u>Friendly Relationship</u>

Some mentoring procedures may need a friendly approach to achieve the desired success. A friend is someone with whom one relates freely on a peer level and enjoys mutual affection, with a free flow of conversation, laughing and crying. A friend is a person with whom one shares cordiality without fear of intimidation or animosity. An experienced mentor should be able to decipher between when a parental attention is needed and when a friendly approach is necessary.

In order for a mentoring relationship to succeed, the mentor must adopt a friendship approach. He must learn to be kind, pleasant, approachable, accessible, supportive, agreeable, and sympathetic to each situation that affects the protégé.

Friendly approach to mentoring would reflect any of the following:

Mate: Friends are usually adopted during academic school age. Some of these friends are study mates who later turned out to be mentors during the process of studying or relating together as classmates.

On the other hand, a mentor and protégé may be age mates. Irrespective of the level of mate, the mentor must not fall short of his/her strength and courage to carry on the relationship.

Sociable: A mentor who is a friend will be sociable and will make a protégé see life as a place of where joy can be attained. A mentor must endeavor to be sociable in order to ease the tension of the mentoring procedures.

Familiar: Since familiarity sometimes brings contempt, a wise mentor should not create unnecessary familiarity which will undermine his ability to oversee his duty in the mentoring procedure.

Companion: A mentor may adopt a protégé as a companion with whom both can share and discuss ideas that are either familiar or strange. The companionship level could create a good ground for the mentor to excel during the process of mentoring.

Approachable and Accessible: A mentor must be approachable and accessible. A person who is not friendly cannot be approachable or accessible. This would create a stumbling block in a mentoring relationship and make a master-servant relationship rather a pure mentoring one. A friend must always be approachable and accessible.

Chapter Eight

Obstacles in Mentoring

In every relationship, be it marriage, leadership, business partnership or friendship, there are impediments that obstruct the relationships. Unless one is realistic about the fact that every relationship has its own impediment and makes a conscious effort to work against it, it will likely occur.

If the causes and prevention of impediments are discussed before a relationship is embarked upon, then one can consciously prevent them from happening. Where the impediment is a habit in one of the parties, then it is necessary to make room for a change to occur, so that that negative element is removed before it creates a problem.

People usually try to ignore or cover up their weaknesses, expecting an automatic disappearance. Since the essence of mentoring is to help to groom and build up, it will be wise for the parties involved to uproot the problem for greater benefit rather than allow it to cause an unforeseen destruction in the future.

Obstacles are negative elements that hinder the progress of a relationship. Such obstacles include: Insecurity, intimidation, procrastination, pride, and fear of promotion, lack of self-control, envy and jealousy.

- **Insecurity (Insincerity to a protégé):** It is a state of mind that makes a person feel insecure and vulnerable, hesitant, uncertain and full of fear of others. Insecurity creates suspicion and falsehood, and rejects the expression of love and assistance, in the midst of honesty and sincerity.
- **Intimidation (Fear of protégé's promotion):** It is a state of fright whereby a person expresses a fear

that the other person's ability to progress will subdue one's position. Intimidation causes one to be terrified, alarmed and petrified when another person is making progress or great achievement. Intimidation does not allow you to accept or acknowledge another person's success.

- **Procrastination:** It is a state of playing delay tactics to deliberately avoid responsibility. Procrastination is a deliberate attempt to frustrate an action that could result in a progress or success. Procrastination is the cause of unfilled promises in relationships.
- **Pride:** It is a feeling of self-importance and self-satisfaction of achievement. Pride makes a person arrogate himself to a position of relegating others with their attitude and language.
- **Familiarity:** It is a state of being well known. The state of over awareness may cause disrespect in a mentoring relationship if a borderline is not drawn.

- **Lack of self-control:** Self-control is a power to restrain and manage one's emotional disposition. Self-control is the ability to switch or exercise authority in times of temperamental provocation.

  Lack of self-control is inability to manage temperamental situations in time of provocation. It is also an expression of deficient disorder in one's thinking faculty that affects the behavior and attitude.
- **Selfish ambition:** Selfishness is to be deficient in consideration for others success or welfare. Ambition is the determination to achieve success or distinction in a chosen field. A person who is selfish in ambition seeks his/her own profit or success without making room for another person.
- **Envy:** Envy is to be resentful towards another person's progress or achievement. An envious person is aroused with the feeling of hatred, bitterness

and destruction at the sight or hearing of another person's success.
- **Jealousy:** Jealousy is to be possessive of another person with a protective attitude and language. A jealous person holds on to something and does not want another person to have access to it.

Chapter Nine

Dynamics of Mentoring

Dynamic is the energy or spirit that motivates the possibility of a concept. The act (not the art or theory but the reality) of mentoring is inspired and driven by three major dynamics—attraction, responsiveness and accountability.

These dynamics are the vitality and the force that propel a desire for mentoring. Thus a person who has been able to attain great heights in his/her life endeavors, either as a successful leader or a successful business person, or a successful personality in certain institutions or organizations, is usually expected to demonstrate distinctive characteristics in their personality.

Besides scholastic, institutional, organizational, managerial, political or governmental achievements, there are factors and attributes that people look out for in a person who has been able to achieve so much in life. The characteristic of the person's achievements must portray the dynamics for mentoring. The dynamics must have the ability to stir up a desire for emulation which is the breeding ground for a mentoring relationship.

This chapter will discuss the three major dynamics of mentoring: Attraction, Responsiveness and Accountability.

i. Attraction

The concept of attraction is one of the three major dynamics that facilitates mentoring. Mentoring is the impartation of knowledge and ability for empowering an individual who seeks to emulate a knowledgeable and experienced personality. One of the dynamics that stirs up a desire for mentoring is attraction.

- Attraction is the unique selling point that attracts everyone to want to buy from a person who sells good things.
- Attraction is the power of conversion that lures a person to emulate a personality.
- Attraction is the spirit that drives a person to entrust his/her life into the hand of another personality.
- Attraction is the vitality that makes a protégé to seek the attention of another personality and regard him/her as a mentor.
- Attraction is a unique element of emulation in considering a mentoring relationship.
- Learning is effective when the element of attraction is present.
- Attraction is the value of qualities that draw people to an achiever to seek a mentoring relationship.

Some of the unique qualities that influence attraction in mentoring relationship include integrity, good listening skills, sincerity, willingness to spend time, communication flow, commitment and competence, experience, accomplishments, maturity, character and behavior.

Spiritual Maturity

Wealth of knowledge and wisdom in the Scripture are part of the major ingredients that motivates attraction for mentoring relationships. The moral lifestyle of a person who is spiritually wealthy is a great attraction that is worthy of emulation. Both parents and individuals, including young and old, will desire to emulate such an individual whose moral lifestyle is spiritually strong and wealthy.

An intending protégé will strive to get connected to a person who is wealthy in knowledge and wisdom, especially if the wealth noted is evidently effective in the person's achievements.

ii. Responsiveness

The ability to give immediate response is a great inspiration that stirs up a good mentoring relationship. To be readily available to meet needs is a unique attribute that facilitates the need for mentoring in many lives. Hence responsiveness is a strong dynamics of mentoring.

Responsiveness is the state of giving immediate answers to arising matters, especially when a help or assistance is called for. It is a mark of honesty and dependability. People always want to entrust their lives into the hands of people who are honest and on whom they can depend.

iii. Accountability

Accountability is one of the dynamics that attracts mentoring relationships. It is the willingness to be responsible for entrustment.

It is the state of rendering account to establish honesty over an assigned responsibility. Mentoring is a process of human management, therefore, it demands accountability.

Anyone seeking a mentoring relationship either as a mentor or a protégé must consider accountability on both sides. The mentor must be able to account for the time invested into the relationship, and the protégé must also endeavor to produce developmental reports to approve the performance of his/her mentor.

Oral and Written Communication

Accountability should be done by both parties on a developmental report sheet and by oral communication or open discussion. Oral communication or open discussion will help each party to express their thoughts freely and also cross-examine matters that need clarification.

Open discussion will enable the expression of thoughts with love and friendliness besides the fatherly or motherly factors that are needed to enhance mentoring relationships.

Written or developmental report sheets help both the mentor and the protégé in a self-examination procedure. It helps the two parties to measure the advancement and pitfalls in the relationship.

Developmental Report and Measurement

The ability to measure the advancement and pitfalls gives room for appropriate corrections to be effected adequately. Since the essence of mentoring is to make amendments and also correct a wrong foundation in a person's life, besides improving one's abilities, it is important that visible approaches be adopted to remove unwanted elements and all manner of impediments that will hinder the purpose of mentoring.

Therefore, for there to be a purported result:

- Targeted goals must be stated in an accountable format (written communication).
- Periodical achievements must be recorded (on a developmental sheet).
- Every correction effected must also be noted for future references against repeated errors (not for intimidation or insecurity but for advancement).

The Song of New Discoveries

Please note that accountability helps to correct past errors. The ability to note your errors will give room to accept correction.

- Reporting your error is not meant to stress your failure nor a cross for crucifixion.
- Reporting your errors brings you into a new level of discovering and writing new songs of development.
- Reporting your errors gives you additions to your wealth of experience.
- Reporting your errors enlightens you on the benefits of accountability:

The songs of rising from failure to the position of experience:

- Failure is just a stopover to revitalize.
- Failure is not the end of the road.
- Failure is the beginning of new thinking.
- Failure is the point of discovering great things.
- Failure is not a cloak of death.
- Failure is not a burial ground.

Therefore, let the little errors that you made become the greatest lessons that led to your promotion. Let your past mistakes add to your wealth of experience from your mentoring relationship.

Then you will have cause to mature and also become an experienced person who can mentor other protégés.

Graduation

At the end of the mentoring program, the protégé must be given a well-done ceremony or graduation. This kind of graduation will enhance the continuity of the mentoring relationship on a higher level or platform. It will also validate and exonerate the mentor and accord him a higher respect in the society.

Chapter Ten

Mentoring Strongmen for Strongholds

What is Mentoring?

Mentoring is a relationship of trust, confidence and respect between an experienced and inexperienced person. It is a process of counseling, guiding, instructing and supporting an inexperienced person to acquire knowledge, values, norms and skills in a particular field.

Mentoring provides a forum for modeling under close supervision on special projects that include: building, correction, discipline, responsibility and accountability. Mentoring is a process of building and developing a person's personality and abilities as well as talents to attain the full potential to fulfill his/her destiny.

Mentoring is also a process of transferring unique abilities and talents to a protégé.

Who is a Mentor?

A mentor is a person who has achieved a professional experience in an area of performance and also has the ability to impact his/her wealth of experience on others.

A mentor is one who has attained a certain measure of influence in a particular field, and is willing to invest his/her wealth of experience and knowledge into another generation of people.

Who is a Strongman/woman?

A strongman/woman is a person who is firm, sturdy, vigorous, effective, formidable, and deep-rooted in his/her position and responsibility. A strongman/woman is also a person who is persuasive, influential and compelling enough to attract followers.

A strongman is also a person who is brilliant, impressive, affective and powerful to motivate others.

In the Home: A strongman is a responsible father, who keeps his home together. A strongwoman is a mother, who builds her home with wisdom and the fear of God.

In the Church: A strongman/woman is a shepherd or minister who keeps feeds and nurtures the flock in the vineyard of our Lord Jesus Christ.

In the Military: A strongman/woman is militant person who exercises authority appropriately to defend and protect a people.

In Leadership: A strongman/woman is a leader who performs his/her duty with determination to achieve targeted goals.

What is a Stronghold?

A stronghold is a place of security and protection. It is a fortress or a refuge. It is a center for a cause of action.

Strongholds include: a home, a church, a military camp or barracks, a hospital, a business organization, an academic institution, etc.

Types of Strongholds

There are godly and ungodly strongholds:

Godly strongholds are related to things pertaining to the plans and purposes of God. Some secular places are part of God's plan and purpose.

Ungodly strongholds are places that have demonic influences. (See details on Strongman and Stronghold in my book: *Pulling Down Satanic Strongholds*).

Mentoring Procedure

The Plan
Mentoring Church Leadership
The Focus: Individual Skills, talents, profession, occupation etc.

The Purpose
To appoint people to occupy the appropriate positions in the church to facilitate effective results

Expectation
For individuals to function effectively in each ministerial department and also fulfill their ambitions

Application
Each protégé must be given assignments that are relevant to his/her skills and talents. Protégés must be allowed to set their own goals and state their desires—what they want to achieve.

Monitoring
Hold developmental and enhancement meeting to examine the quality of work done and analyze the progress made as a result of the mentoring relationship.

Progress Report

Set up Goals: Periodical goals—weekly and monthly goals

Hitting the Targets: Periodical targets

Results: developments, hindrances and successes

Bibliography

Engstrom, Ted W. 1989. *The Fine Art of Mentoring*. Newburgh, Indiana: Trinity Press.

Schultz Steve and Gaborit Chris. 1996. *Mentoring and Fathering*. Christian International Ministries, Santa Rosa Beach, Florida.

Wise, Terry S. 1999. *Mentoring Relationships*. Indiana, USA: Avalon Press.

Pauline Walley School of Intensive Training For Ministry and Leadership Equipment (PW-SITME)

The Pauline Walley School of Intensive Training for Ministry Equipment is an institution for training leaders, individuals and church groups. It is an intensive practical training center where people are taught to build their images and personalities, improve their ministry skills and abilities, develop their talents and gifts, minister to self, family members, friends and to church or fellowship members. In the process of training, people are also taught to be equipped for ministration and to face the battle of life as it is in the ministry.

The areas of study are:

School of Deliverance (SOD)
School of Strategic Prayer (SSP)
School of Tactical Evangelism (STE)
School of Mentoring and Leadership (SML)
School of the Gifts of the Holy Spirit (SGHS)
School of the Prophets (SOP)

The Pauline Walley School of Intensive Training programs are organized and held in different parts of the world at various times. At seminar levels, one week or two weeks of intensive training are organized to help leaders and ministers or church/fellowship groups to establish various arms of church ministry and also equip their members for such purposes.

Bi-weekly intensive training programs and one-year certificate courses are readily available in Bronx, New York and other regions based on request. If you are interested in hosting any of these programs in your region or country or church/ministry, please contact us. *See details of our contact information and website on the back page.*

Christian Books By
DR. PAULINE WALLEY

THE AUTHORITY OF AN OVERCOMER: YOU CAN HAVE IT . . . I HAVE IT
The Authority of An Overcomer shares the real-life testimony of a day-to-day experience with the Lord Jesus Christ. It encourages you to apply the Word of God to every facet of your life, such as sleeping and waking with Jesus, walking and talking with Jesus, and dining with Him as you would with your spouse or a friend.

SOMEBODY CARES . . . CARES FOR YOU . . . CARES FOR ME
Somebody Cares . . . Cares for you . . . Cares for Me talks about the care that the Lord Almighty has for every one of us. It teaches you to care for other people and exercise tolerance towards their shortcomings. You will learn the importance of love and the true meaning as you read this book

RECEIVE AND MAINTAIN YOUR DELIVERANCE ON LEGAL GROUNDS.

Many people go from one prayer house to another, from the general practitioner to the specialist, from one minister to the pope; and from one chapel to another church, with the same mission, aiming for the same expectation, yet, never hitting the target. Why? Many people lack the knowledge of maintaining their healing and deliverance. This book: *Receive and Maintain Your Deliverance on Legal Grounds,* will teach you to understand how to maintain what you receive from God.

ANGER: GET RID OF IT . . . YOU CAN OVERCOME IT

Anger is one of the many problems that many seek to resolve but lack the solution. Many have resigned their fate to it, thinking that it is a natural phenomenon. This book teaches about the causes of anger and how to uproot them to receive your healing.

THE POWER OF THE SPOKEN WORD

There is a purpose for which we speak, and when we speak, we expect something to happen in order for the purpose of the utterance to be fulfilled. This book teaches you to exercise your authority so that the word that you speak would be manifested effectively.

THE HOLY SPIRIT: THE UNIQUENESS OF HIS PRESENCE.

The presence of the Holy Spirit highlights the difference between the gifts of the Spirit, the presence of God and the visitation of the Holy Spirit. In this book you will learn to enjoy the delightful presence of the Holy Spirit in your spiritual walk.

THE HOLY SPIRIT: MAINTAIN HIS PRESENCE IN TRIALS AND TEMPTATIONS

This book teaches you how to maintain the presence of God, especially in trials and temptations. Oftentimes, when Christians go through difficult situations, they think they are alone. But that need not be. You can enter the presence of the Holy Spirit in difficult times and witness His Power to strengthen you and turn your situations around.

PROGRESSIVE ACHIEVEMENT: RECEIVE IT; MAINTAIN IT

This book teaches you how to move on continuously and overcome obstacles that usually frustrate prosperity. It enlightens you about the various types of progress that may come your way and how to manage them. It also encourages you to overcome failure and disappointment. The book also helps you to understand the concept of continuity and progressiveness as part of the characteristics of the Holy Spirit.

THE HOLY SPIRIT: POWER OF THE TONGUE

In recent times many people have been seeking instant power and prophetic manifestations. Christians and ministers are indulging in all sorts of practices to demonstrate some special abilities to attract public attention. This book, *Power of the Tongue*, discusses the various powers and anointing(s) at work. It will help you to decipher between the Holy Spirit power and satanic powers. It will also teach you about the various anointing(s) that exist and how you can reach out for the genuine one.

PULLING DOWN SATANIC STRONGHOLDS: WAR AGAINST EVIL SPIRITS

Many Christians are under satanic attacks and influences, but very few people understand what the actual problems are. Some believe in God but have no idea that there is anything like the satanic realm, yet they are under satanic torments. This book, *Pulling Down Satanic Strongholds*, enlightens you on some of the operations of the devil. It will help you know when an activity being performed around you is of the devil. This knowledge will strengthen you in prayer and equip you against the wiles of the enemy.

WHEN SATAN WENT TO CHURCH?

Many people fear the devil more than they fear God. At the mention of Satan or demons, they are threatened to death. Yet they are complacent in their own ways and yield to sin easily. Let the fear of God grip you and not the fear of Satan. This book enlightens you on the activities of the enemy within and around the church, the home and the Christian community. It helps you to identify battles and to put on your armor of warfare against the enemy. It also encourages you to hold firm the shield of faith. May the Lord enlighten your eyes of understanding as you read this book.

SOLUTION: DELIVERANCE MINISTRATION TO SELF AND OTHERS

Since the death of Jesus Christ on the cross, humans have been given the opportunity to experience and encounter the joy of salvation. However, lack of knowledge has kept the world in the dark and deprived them of the importance of Christianity. This book, *Solution: Deliverance Ministration to Self and Others*, portrays just what the title says. It teaches you to understand the intricacies of deliverance ministration and to avoid the dangerous practices that have discouraged others. Read it and you will be blessed as never before.

Subscription

GOSPEL SONGS ON CASSETTE
Overcomers' Expression
Send Your Power
Vessels of Worship
Poetic Expression

BOOKS
All the books listed can be ordered
CONTACT: For Ministration

WEST AFRICA
Pauline Walley School of Deliverance
P.O. Box MS 301, Mile-Seven, Accra, Ghana.
Tel/Fax: (233) 400907, 403054, 403063 or 404184

UNITED KINGDOM
Pauline Walley Christian Communications
P.O. Box 4673, London SE1 4UQ.
Tel: (44) 794-769-7867

UNITED STATES
Pauline Walley Christian Communications
P. O. Box 250, Bronx, NY 10467
Telephone (718) 652-2916/Fax (718) 405-2035

Email: drpauline@paulinewalley.org
paulinewalley@optonline.net
Website: www.school-of-deliverance.com
www.paulinewalley.org www.overcomershouse.com

About the School of Mentoring and Leadership

Everyone has talents and abilities that need to be developed in order for a person to achieve an ambition. Many people are bedeviled by fulfilled dreams and are wallowing in familiar oppression and depression. This book will help you to locate and choose a mentor, who will help you to discover and develop your abilities that will lead you into fulfilling your ambition. This course will teach and draw you closer to your destiny. Stay blessed and enjoy the *Act of Mentoring*.

About Dr. Pauline Walley

Dr. Pauline Walley is an ordained prophet-evangelist who teaches the **Word of God** with dramatic demonstrations. She is anointed by the Holy Spirit to teach the gospel of healing and deliverance and to impart the message of love and joy to the people.

Dr. Pauline travels to various parts of the world, ministering in churches, crusades, revivals and seminars in various academic institutions, as well as speaking to professional bodies. She is also talented in writing, drama, poetry and composing songs. Some of her musical works are also on record. She is also the author of twelve other books.

Dr. Pauline is the President of Pauline Walley Evangelistic Ministries and Christian Communications as well the Director of the School of Intensive Training for Leadership Equipment that includes the School of Deliverance in New York. The School trains ministers, groups and individuals all over the world. Before her call into full-time ministry, Pauline Walley, who holds a Masters degree in Journalism, was one of the few women in Sports Journalism. Dr. Pauline holds her PhD in Pulpit Communications and Expository Preaching.

ISBN: 0-9724540-2-0

CPSIA information can be obtained at www.ICGtesting.com
Printed in the USA
269618BV00001B/26/A